A Terrible Tale of a Dreaded Dragon

by Burt Liebert

Baker's Plays
c/o Samuel French, Inc.
45 West 25 Street
New York, NY 10010
bakersplays.com

NOTICE

This book is offered for sale at the price quoted only on the understanding that, if any additional copies of the whole or any part are necessary for its production, such additional copies will be purchased. The attention of all purchasers is directed to the following: this work is fully protected under the copyright laws of the United States of America, the British Commonwealth, including Canada, and all other countries of the Copyright Union. Violations of the Copyright Law are punishable by fine or imprisonment, or both. The copying or duplication of this work or any part of this work, by hand or by any process, is an infringement of the copyright and will be vigorously prosecuted.

This play may not be produced by amateurs or professionals for public or private performance without first submitting application for performing rights. Licensing fees are due on all performances whether for charity or gain, or whether admission is charged or not. Since performance of this play without the payment of the licensing fee renders anybody participating liable to severe penalties imposed by the law, anybody acting in this play should be sure, before doing so, that the licensing fee has been paid. Professional rights, reading rights, radio broadcasting, television and all mechanical rights, etc. are strictly reserved. Application for performing rights should be made directly to BAKER'S PLAYS.

No one shall commit or authorize any act or omission by which the copyright of, or the right to copyright, this play may be impaired. No one shall make any changes in this play for the purpose of production.

Publication of this play does not imply availability for performance. Both amateurs and professionals considering a production are strongly advised in their own interest to apply to Baker's Plays for written permission before starting rehearsals, advertising, or booking a theatre.

Whenever the play is produced, the author's name must be carried in all publicity, advertising and programs. Also, the following notice must appear on all printed programs, "Produced by special arrangement with Baker's Plays."

Licensing fees for A TERRIBLE TALE OF A DREADED DRAGON are based on a per performance rate and payable one week in advance of the production.

Please consult the Baker's Plays website at www.bakersplays.com or our current print catalogue for up to date licensing fee information.

CITIZENS OF THE KINGDOM

HAN
HER CHILD
SHENG
TSUNG
LAO
HAI

THE ROYAL FIRST SECRETARY
THE ROYAL GENERAL OF ALL THE ARMY
THE SOLDIER
PENG, A STRANGER
THE ROYAL HERALD
THE GREAT EMPRESS
THE GREAT EMPEROR
THE DREADED DRAGON
THE CHILDREN IN THE AUDIENCE.

AUTHOR'S NOTE: Although the play was written for six citizens, it can be performed with as few as two, or as many as the stage will hold. The dialogue may be reassigned as desired. The parts of the Royal First Secretary, the Herald, and the Dragon were written for actresses, but can be performed by men by changing "she" to "he."

SCENES:

The Village Center in a far-away place.
Later in the Great Purple Forest
The Village Center Again

A TERRIBLE TALE
OF A DREADED DRAGON

(The setting is The Village Center, in a far-away place. A brightly-colored banner or sign on a stout pole signals that this is the city of the Emperor and Empress. Two thrones are set up, one higher than the other. [The Great Palace may be seen in the background. Houses may be added, and Citizens may enter and exit through their own doors, but all this is not necessary.]

At rise, the stage is empty. Opening MUSIC swells to crescendo as the CITIZENS enter from various directions. THEY walk about the stage in confusion and fear.)

CHAN. Have you seen it?

TSUNG. No

SHENG. No.

HAI. They say it was last seen in the rice fields, eating all the good rice that we spent the whole season growing.

LAO. Better it eat the rice than...

ALL CITIZENS. Oooooooh!

SHENG. I heard it was seen in the Great Purple Forest.

LAO. Everyone knows it is by the Emerald Lake, drinking half the water in one great gulp.

TSUNG. I know it is in the rice fields.

HAI. Nothing of the kind. It was last seen wandering in the Far Blue Hills.

SHENG. The Great Purple Forest.

LAO. Emerald Lake.
HAI. Far Blue Hills.
TSUNG. The rice fields.

(*During this scene, the ROYAL FIRST SECRETARY, the ROYAL GENERAL OF ALL THE ARMY, and the SOLDIER enter. The First Secretary wears a huge medallion of office. She smiles craftily as she observes the Citizens' fear and confusion. The General smiles weakly, for he shares the Citizens' fear. The Soldier stands fearfully, sword in hand.*)

TSUNG. (*Indicating the audience.*) Perhaps these children know where it is.
CHAN. Let us ask them.
SHENG. (*Turning to the audience.*) Have you seen -- the -- the Dreaded Dragon?

(*All CITIZENS approach the audience and ask them "Have you seen the Dragon? Do you know where it is?"*)

LAO. It is a huge beast, with claws like those of an eagle.
HAI. Only longer.
CHAN. And sharper.
LAO. And the teeth of a great yellow tiger.
SHENG. Only far more terrible.
TSUNG. And its favorite food is...
ALL CITIZENS. Us!
LAO. If you see it, please tell us, that we may run as fast as our legs will carry us.
FIRST SECRETARY. The Dreadful Dragon was last seen

-- coming this way!

(The CITIZENS scream and run about the stage in confusion, bumping into each other.   Finally all CITIZENS exit in various directions.)

FIRST SECRETARY. Ah, my good General, our plan is working, thanks to that Dreaded Dragon.

GENERAL. The people are afraid to gather the rice. They fear they will meet the Dragon in the rice fields.

GENERAL. They fear the Dragon will pounce on them and gobble them up.

FIRST SECRETARY. It is well known that dragons eat people.

GENERAL. The citizens cower in their homes.

FIRST SECRETARY. Or huddle together here by the Empress' throne.

GENERAL. So the rice fields are deserted.

FIRST SECRETARY. That means we can pick all the rice.

GENERAL. Because nobody will be there to see us.

FIRST SECRETARY. We can keep all the rice for ourselves.

GENERAL. Or sell it at the market.

FIRST SECRETARY. And make ourselves rich.

GENERAL. And nobody will ever know.

FIRST SECRETARY. Nobody will be near the rice fields to see us.

GENERAL. Everyone is frightened of that Dreaded Dragon. *(Suddenly remembering, he seeks safety behind the SOLDIER.)* So am I!

FIRST SECRETARY. Nonsense! You are the Royal

General. When we go into the fields to gather the rice you can have the entire army to protect us.

GENERAL. (*Pointing to the Soldier.*)   But this is the entire army. (*The SOLDIER gives a half-hearted little salute.*)

FIRST SECRETARY. And what a splendid army it is! You, Soldier! You are not afraid to face a dragon, are you?

SOLDIER. (*His knees shaking.*) Nnnno, Ssssir.

FIRST SECRETARY. There, you see! This fine army will protect us from that Dragon. We will meet in the rice field this afternoon.

GENERAL. THIS afternoon? But the DRAGON may be in the rice field. Why not wait until tomorrow?

FIRST SECRETARY. No! The crop is ripe. We will pick all the rice this afternoon. Bring the largest baskets you can find.

GENERAL. (*With great lack of enthusiasm.*) Very well.

FIRST SECRETARY. (*To the Soldier.*) You may stay here and guard the city. The Empress will pass by soon. (*Full of her own importance.*) We must join the Royal Procession. If the Dragon appears -- do your duty!

GENERAL. Do your duty!

(*The GENERAL and the FIRST SECRETARY exit. The SOLDIER remains "on guard," expecting the Dragon to appear at any moment. HE speaks to the audience, trembling.*)

SOLDIER. Do your duty! Do your duty! How can I do my duty against a dragon? Do you know how big those beasts are? How fierce? I am told they have claws like... It is known they have teeth like... It is not easy being an entire army!

(Enter PENG, a pleasant-looking lad, strolling along, unseen by the Soldier. HE sees the Soldier, comes up behind him, and in a friendly way taps him on the shoulder. The SOLDIER, startled, jumps back and falls over the throne [or into the arms of Peng].)

SOLDIER. Eeeeh!
PENG. Did I frighten you?
SOLDIER. Frighten me? Why, you nearly scared me to death!
PENG. I only tapped you on the shoulder, very lightly -- like this --

(HE taps the Soldier on the shoulder again, and again the SOLDIER jumps back, startled, and falls over the throne.)

SOLDIER. Eeeeh! That's what I mean. It's very frightening to be tapped on the shoulder like that.
PENG. But I meant no harm. I'm a very friendly person.
SOLDIER. How was I to know that?
PENG. *(Appeals to the audience.)* Now, I ask you. Did I do anything so terribly frightening? What do you think?

(If audience reaction is "no.")   *(If audience reaction is "yes.")*

PENG. There! you see!   SOLDIER. There! you see.

(The SOLDIER and PENG may ad lib briefly, depending on the audience reaction.)

SOLDIER. You are a stranger here, so you do not know what I know.

PENG. Know? Know what?

SOLDIER. Aha! You don't know about the -- (*He hesitates to say it -- the very word is terrifying.*) the -- the Dreaded Dragon!

PENG. Oh, I should love to see a dragon. (*A loud GONG is heard offstage. The SOLDIER snaps to attention.*)

SOLDIER. The Empress!

(*The EMPRESS enters, accompanied by the ROYAL FIRST SECRETARY, the ROYAL HERALD, who carries a gong, The GENERAL, and -- oh, yes -- the EMPEROR. The Emperor is a pleasant little fellow who likes everybody, but is completely dominated by his wife, the Empress. He may greet individual children in the audience as he enters.*)

EMPEROR. Hello... I'm the Great Emperor. Do you like my kingdom? I hope you have a nice visit here. Isn't it awful about that Dragon! (*HE continues to chat with the children until the EMPRESS clears her throat meaningfully and scowls at him.*) 'Scuse me!

(*HE hurries to take his place on the lower throne. The EMPRESS sits on the higher throne. The CITIZENS enter, wailing with grief, stepping cautiously, looking around fearfully as they go.*)

CITIZENS. (*May be chanted or sung as a CHORUS with solos.*)

POOR ME! POOR ME! OH, SEE MY MISERY!
TO FACE THAT BEAST WOULD TAKE AT LEAST
A HUNDRED INFANTRY!

I SEE, I SEE, THIS IS THE END OF ME!
TO FACE THAT BEAST WOULD TAKE AT LEAST
A THOUSAND CAVALRY!

POOR ME! POOR ME! POOR ME, POOR ME, POOR ME!
TO FACE THAT BEAST WOULD TAKE AT LEAST
SOME HUGE ARTILLERY!

(The HERALD strikes the GONG, and the song ends.)

EMPRESS. *(Pointing to the Soldier.)* General! Have that
man report.

EMPEROR. Yes, excellent idea, my Pet. Have that man
report at once.

GENERAL. *(Full of importance.)* Yes, Your Majesty --
er, Majesties. Harumph! *(To the Soldier.)* Er, ah -- attention!
*(The SOLDIER, already at attention, gives a shake and resumes
the same position.)* Yes, ah -- report!

SOLDIER. *(With great importance -- a stupendous
announcement.)* Sir, I have nothing to report!

GENERAL. Any sign of the -- ah -- enemy?

SOLDIER. No, Sir.

GENERAL. Excellent! Your Majesty -- er -- Majesties --
he has nothing to --

EMPRESS. I heard him.

EMPEROR. Yes, yes. Quite clearly. We heard.

EMPRESS. Herald, read my royal proclamation.

EMPEROR. But, my love, we have read the proclamation

one hundred seventy-eight times already. And nobody has volunteered yet.

EMPRESS. Read it again. Surely there must be one brave person in all the kingdom.

HERALD. (*Reading from a scroll.*) I, Empress of all the land as far as the eye can see, and a long way beyond that, do hereby decree that whoever shall rid my kingdom of the Dreadful Dragon shall receive a great reward.

EMPRESS. Who shall volunteer to rid the kingdom of this terrible beast? (*All CITIZENS tremble and shake their heads.*) Come, are there no courageous fellows in all the kingdom?

PENG. (*Kneels before the Emperor and Empress.*) Your Majesties!

EMPRESS. Who is this -- person?

PENG. Great Emperor -- Great Empress. I come from a distant land.

EMPRESS. And what would you do in our kingdom?

PENG. I go from place to place, for something seems to say to me: *see what is over there. Find out more.*

EMPRESS. Have you heard about the Dreaded Dragon?

PENG. Tell me more about it.

HERALD. (*Throughout the next lines, the FIRST SECRETARY smiles, while the others tremble.*)

HERALD. He is a huge beast, with scales as hard as the finest bronze.

GENERAL. Fire comes out of his mouth and nose, scorching everything in his path.

CHAN. Since the Dragon entered our kingdom, we live in constant fear for our lives.

TSUNG. The Dragon has been seen sneaking about -- waiting to grab some poor citizen.

SHENG. And turn that unfortunate person into his dinner.

HAI. Everyone knows that dragons -- eat people!

LAO. We dare not go into the forest to gather wood.

(*Each of these statements brings about an outburst of fear and trembling.*)

CHAN. For fear the Dragon may be somewhere close.

HAI. So we cannot cook our food or heat our homes against the hard winter frost.

CHAN. Our fruit withers on the trees.

HAI. We dare not go into the fields to gather rice.

TSUNG. For fear of the Dragon.

CHAN. So we are starving.

LAO. With nothing to put in the rice bowl.

(*A NOISE is heard offstage. The CITIZENS scream and hide behind the GENERAL, who abandons them to hide behind the SOLDIER.*)

PENG. (*Looking offstage.*) It was but a limb falling from a dead tree. Is the Dragon really that terrible?

CHAN. My husband says he is bigger than a house!

TSUNG. My neighbor says he is bigger than the tallest tree!

SHENG. My brother's wife's cousin says that he is bigger than -- bigger than -- bigger than that!

PENG. To rid the kingdom of such a beast would be a fine adventure! But how? (*He thinks visibly, then makes a decision.*) I shall set out at once. I'm sure I shall think of something.)

FIRST SECRETARY. (*Casts an angry glance at PENG.*) Do you not see the danger in such an undertaking?

PENG. Of course. Not to recognize danger is only to be foolish.

GENERAL. Then you will give up this impossible task?

PENG. No. Courage is knowing the danger and feeling the fear -- then going ahead in spite of the fear.

LAO. What a pity for one so fair to die so young!

CHAN. For such a dragon, he would be but a single bite.

PENG. But tell me where I may find the beast, and I shall begin immediately.

HERALD. The Dragon is often seen in the Great Purple Forest.

(Mention of the Great Purple Forest again strikes fear into all the CITIZENS. They wait until silenced by the GONG. A sword is brought on and ceremoniously presented to PENG.)

PENG. *(Sings.)*
I'M GOING TO GET THE DRAGON
AND I AM NOT A-BRAGGIN'.
I'LL TWIST HIS TAIL, HE'LL LET OUT A WAIL,
AND I'LL CARRY HIM OFF ON A WAGON!

(HE goes into a little dance, as the chorus sings.)

CHORUS.
HE'S GOING TO GET THE DRAGON.
AND HE IS NOT A-BRAGGIN'.
HE'LL TWIST HIS TAIL, HE'LL LET OUT A WAIL,
AND HE'LL CARRY HIM OFF ON A WAGON!

(THEY all lift PENG on their shoulders and sing together.)

WE'RE GOING TO GET THE DRAGON
AND WE ARE NOT A-BRAGGIN'.
WE'LL TWIST HIS TAIL, HE'LL LET OUT A WAIL,
AND WE'LL CARRY HIM OFF ON A WAGON!

PENG. I presume you will all come with me -- to show me the way to the Great Purple Forest.

(Suddenly fearful again, THEY let PENG down and shrink away from him. PENG goes to everyone on stage individually, but each one backs away from him and shakes his head.)

Just to the EDGE of the Forest... I shall face the Dragon alone ...only a short distance...

(One by one, everyone but PENG exits, the Royal Procession pretending great dignity, the CITIZENS openly fearful. Everyone may ad lib excuses, such as:)

EMPRESS. I must attend matters of state!
EMPEROR. Yes, yes -- of state.
GENERAL. I must review my army.
SOLDIER. You heard the General. I must report to the parade ground.
FIRST SECRETARY. I must advise the Empress.
HERALD. I must polish the gong!
PENG. *(He finally turns to the audience.)* Who will come with me to the edge of the Forest?

(HE takes the VOLUNTEERS up on the stage, and together they begin. [The object is to encourage as

many children as possible to participate. If there are too many for the stage to hold, PENG may direct them to "stand up and sing along at your seats.")

Now sing with me -- WE'RE GOING TO GET THE DRAGON!

(He accents "GO," "GET," and "DRAG" by taking a step on each word. HE leads the CHILDREN around and about the stage, conducting their song:)

WE'RE GOING TO GET THE DRAGON,
AND WE ARE NOT A-BRAGGIN'.
WE'LL TWIST HIS TAIL, HE'LL LET OUT A WAIL,
AND WE'LL CARRY HIM OFF ON A WAGON!

(This can continue as long as the CHILDREN are enthusiastic, but not rowdy. PENG can punctuate the song by giving commands between verses, such as "loud — hum — whisper — whistle." With a gesture he stops the singing. [A stage hand brings on a purple tree and sets it up on stage, removing one of the thrones as he exits.] PENG doesn't see it. [In the original production, the TREES were played by actors, who doubled as CITIZENS. In another production, the TREES were cut out of pressboard.] The LIGHT gradually turns purple.)

PENG. I wonder when we'll get to the Great Purple Forest.

([Another tree is brought on, then more, and the Palace

set is cleared]. PENG continues to ask, as he treks on,
"I wonder where that Great Purple Forest can be,"
until the children point to the trees.)

Oh, we're there -- I mean -- we're here. The Dreadful Dragon
must be dreadfully close. You had better go back now. You'll
be safe if you stay in your seats. Just stay seated, and the
Dragon can't hurt you.

(HE "herds" the children back to their seats and faces
the Forest.)

I must admit I am a little more fearful than I thought I would
be. But I suppose -- without something to fear -- there would
be no adventure. Bigger than a house -- bigger than the tallest
tree -- scales harder than --- fire from his -- What can I do
against such a beast? I suppose this is what they call a
challenge. Well, no challenge, no adventure, eh?

(HE steels himself for the task ahead and presses on,
sword in hand. HE circles the stage a few times,
gingerly looking for the DRAGON. Twice he thinks he
hears a sound and jumps fearfully, but each turns out to
be a false alarm. Then a strange SOUND is heard, of
deep breathing -- somewhat like a roar. The SOUND
gets louder and louder.)

I think I hear -- yes, I definitely hear --

(HE looks cautiously about, sword in hand, fearful but
ready to do battle. Enter the DREADED DRAGON.
PENG has his back to the DRAGON, looking in every

direction but the right one. Except for his tail, which curls behind, the DRAGON is no larger than an average person, or even smaller. HE walks on his hind legs, using his front paws as you and I use our arms. I'm sorry, dear audience, but no fire can be seen about his nostrils. HE sees Peng, stops his heavy breathing, and studies PENG carefully. Cautious but curious, HE approaches PENG from behind. PENG makes a wide circle, looking for the Dragon. The DRAGON follows behind. Finally, in a friendly manner, the DRAGON taps PENG in the side with his elbow. Startled, PENG jumps, frightening the DRAGON. THEY jump apart, each staring at the other for a moment. Finally, PENG, remembering what he came for, with a great war cry, rushes at the DRAGON.)

Now, dreadful beast, prepare to meet they doom!

(The DRAGON, seeing PENG rush at him with a sword, flees in panic, PENG in hot pursuit. After a chase around the trees, the DRAGON sinks to the floor in fear, covers his head with his front paws, and kneels there, shaking. PENG backs away, not knowing what to do next.)

Aren't you going to fight?

(The DRAGON shakes his head "no." The DRAGON does not speak, but understands what is said, and pantomimes responses, nodding "yes" and "no," shrugging his shoulders, and otherwise communicating. He is a bit like an oversized puppy. He gestures to

Peng with his arm "come here." At first PENG hesitates, then gingerly approaches the DRAGON, who gets down on all fours and rubs his head against PENG's leg. Slowly PENG discovers the GREAT SECRET:)

Why -- why, you're not such a terrible beast!

(The DRAGON rolls over on his back with all four legs in the air, and PENG throws his sword away.)

I don't need this!

(HE pets the DRAGON's tummy as one would a dog's. With each of Pengs's statements, the DRAGON shakes his head "no.")

And you're not nearly as big as a tree. Or even a house. In fact -- I think you're a friendly little fellow!

(The DRAGON gets up, takes PENG's hands, and dances him around the stage, PENG laughing, the DRAGON filled with the joy of a new friend.)

Why, I've never danced with a dragon. This is the finest adventure I've ever had! *(He thinks for a moment.)* I wonder who else would like to dance with a dragon. *(To the audience.)* Why, here are all the children who came with me to the edge of the Great Purple Forest. Perhaps THEY would like to dance with the Dragon. Would anyone here like to dance with a dragon?

(If only a few children volunteer, THEY may come up on stage, take the DRAGON's hands, and dance around with him. If many volunteer, the DRAGON and PENG give each child a merry twirl or two. The dance over, PENG and the DRAGON usher the CHILDREN back to their seats and return to the stage to resume.)

But if you're such a merry fellow, why do you lurk about to carry off our good citizens?

(The DRAGON pantomimes, "Who, me?")

Haven't you been stealing into the Village to carry off the people for your dinner?

(The DRAGON attempts to "carry off" PENG, but collapses under the weight, PENG on top of him.)

I say, you're not the strongest dragon in the world. Why, you couldn't carry off anyone if you tried.

(Sadly, the DRAGON agrees.)

Come back with me, my friend. We must tell the people they needn't live in fear.

(The DRAGON shakes his head "no" and hides behind a tree. He knows how people feel about dragons.)

But they dare not gather wood or pick their crops for fear of you.

(Sadly, the DRAGON refuses again.)

But the people are starving with nothing to put in their rice bowls.

(The DRAGON hangs his head, gives a great sigh, then slowly, reluctantly, starts to go with PENG. But before they can take a few steps, VOICES are heard offstage. PENG and the DRAGON hide. The FIRST SECRETARY, The GENERAL, and The SOLDIER enter. The SOLDIER staggers under the weight of two huge, heavy baskets on the ends of a pole, each piled high with rice. The GENERAL and the SOLDIER walk cautiously, hands on swords, looking out for the Dragon, but the FIRST SECRETARY walks boldly. The GENERAL walks painfully, one hand on his aching back.)

FIRST SECRETARY. Step quickly. It is late, and we must hurry to the marketplace.

GENERAL. I have worked all afternoon picking rice. I cannot step quickly. I am tired and my back aches.

FIRST SECRETARY. You, the Royal General of All the Army, tired just from gathering a bit of rice. I am not tired.

GENERAL. You did not gather rice. You did not spend the whole afternoon bending down and standing up, and bending down again! Oh, my poor back!

FIRST SECRETARY. I am the Empress' First Secretary. I do not pick rice.

GENERAL. Well, I am the Royal General of the Entire Army. And I had to do all the work.

FIRST SECRETARY. Nonsense! You had the entire

army helping you.

GENERAL. Well, we have picked all the rice there is.

FIRST SECRETARY. We shall bring it to the market.

GENERAL. We shall sell it all.

FIRST SECRETARY. It will bring a great price. We shall be rich.

PENG. (*Stepping into the open.*) So that was your scheme! You are stealing the people's rice. You are starving them to make yourselves rich!

FIRST SECRETARY. (*Amazed to find herself discovered.*) It is death to spy on the Empress' First Secretary. Seize him!

(*THEY are about to pounce on PENG when the DRAGON shows himself. The GENERAL, in terror, jumps into the arms of the SOLDIER, or hides behind him.*)

GENERAL. The Dragon! The Dragon!

FIRST SECRETARY. You fool! Can you not see that it is but a little Dragon -- harmless and defenseless? Tie them to a tree.

(*Swords drawn, the GENERAL and the SOLDIER start after PENG and the DRAGON.*)

FIRST SECRETARY. Catch them! Hurry, you fools, don't let them get away! (*SHE continues to urge them on, as they chase PENG and the DRAGON, finally catching them and tying them to a tree.*)

GENERAL. You knew the Dragon was small and harmless. That is why you were so courageous. Why did you not tell me?

FIRST SECRETARY. Because you cannot keep a thing to yourself. Everyone but me had to fear the Dragon. Everyone else had to be afraid to go into the fields. Or else my scheme would be ruined.

SOLDIER. (*Slowly realizes what is happening.*) Excuse me, Sir, but if you sell all the rice, what will the people eat this winter?

FIRST SECRETARY. That is not your affair, Soldier.

SOLDIER. But the people will go hungry.

GENERAL. A good soldier asks no questions.

FIRST SECRETARY. A good soldier obeys orders.

GENERAL. A good soldier tells no tales.

FIRST SECRETARY. Now it is too late to sell the rice today. Let us take it to my chamber overnight. We can sell it tomorrow.

GENERAL. Then we can return.

FIRST SECRETARY. To make sure these two do not tell what they have seen.

GENERAL. Soldier! You are to guard the prisoners carefully.

FIRST SECRETARY. If they are not here when we return, you will lose your head! (*She gestures, her fingers across her throat.*)

GENERAL. Your head!

(*HE repeats her gesture, picks up the baskets of rice and, struggling under the weight, exits with the FIRST SECRETARY. [If an INTERMISSION is desired, it can be inserted here. Or you may prefer to break later, when the scene changes. When the scene begins again, PENG and the DRAGON are still tied, and the SOLDIER is pacing up and down, talking to himself, deeply troubled and confused.*)

SOLDIER. A good soldier obeys orders. I was ordered to guard the prisoners...

PENG. But if they sell all the rice, what will the people eat?

SOLDIER. Silence! The prisoner is not to speak. But if they sell all the rice, what will the people eat? (*To the audience.*) Could my General and my First Secretary be doing something bad?

PENG. You saw them steal the people's rice.

SOLDIER. I said silence! I saw them steal the people's rice. I shall guard the prisoners, then I shall tell the people what happened to their food... But a good soldier tells no tales... What if – ? How can I – ? But a good soldier asks no questions. But I cannot let the people starve. I shall let them go! (*HE starts to untie the ropes, hesitates.*) But if the prisoners are not here when the others return, I shall lose my head. And losing my head may be extremely – uncomfortable! (*HE turns towards the audience.*) I wonder what I should do...? (*[The SOLDIER may ad lib in reaction to the audience.]*) I seem to hear voices saying "Let them go. Let them go." I don't want to be a bad soldier. (*As the struggle within reaches a climax.*) Yes, I do! (*Having finally made a decision, he rushes to PENG and the DRAGON and unties their bonds.*) Come! Let us tell the people where their rice is hidden.

PENG. And free them from their fear of the Dragon!

(*THEY rush off as the LIGHTS fade. If desired, the INTERMISSION may be located here. The CITIZENS can be heard singing "Poor me." When the LIGHTS*

*come on again, we are back in the village. The
EMPEROR and EMPRESS, and EVERYONE from the
Village are on stage. The FIRST SECRETARY and the
GENERAL exchange sly glances. The OTHERS are
motionless, lost in gloom.)*

SHENG. Much time has passed since the stranger left.
TSUNG. He will never return.
CHAN. No one returns from the place of the Dragon.
HAI. They say the Dragon is larger than the Purple
Mountains far to the west.
LAO. He is so fierce -- just to look at him will freeze the
blood in the bravest man's veins.
A CHILD. *(Glancing offstage, she runs to get a better
look.)* Mother, I see some people coming. *(EVERYONE looks
offstage.)*
TSUNG. I think -- I think it is the stranger!
SHENG. There is someone with him.
LAO. It is the soldier.
CHAN. There is a third person.
CHILD. It is some -- thing.
TSUNG. It is a beast.
SHENG. What kind of beast?
CHILD. It is the DRAGON! *(The CITIZENS scream and
back away.)*
CHAN. The stranger and our Soldier have slain the
Dragon! *(General cheer.)*
SHENG. They are carrying the Dragon between them.
TSUNG. No, they have captured the Dragon. They are
leading him back -- in strong chains.
CHILD. The Dragon is not in chains. He is walking
between them.

LAO. They are coming closer.

HAI. They are here. (*Enter PENG, the SOLDIER, and the DRAGON. The CITIZENS shrink away in fear.*)

PENG. Good Citizens, do not fear the Dragon. He will not harm you. See -- he is only a very small Dragon, and quite friendly.

(*Slowly, seeing what a small DRAGON he is, and reassured by PENG, the CITIZENS cautiously approach the DRAGON, led by the CHILD. The DRAGON gives a little sneeze, and everyone retreats again. Then, little by little, they gather courage and approach the DRAGON once more.*)

FIRST SECRETARY. Seize the Dragon! He must be put to death.

PENG. No! Wait! Let me tell you...

GENERAL. This beast will destroy us all if we do not rid the kingdom of him.

FIRST SECRETARY. And this young stranger is a spy! I caught him spying on me in the Great Purple Forest.

PENG. That's not true.

GENERAL. Great Empress! We cannot permit spies to pass among us. And this soldier is a traitor. He was ordered to guard the enemy, and he let them go.

SOLDIER. But there is a reason, your Majesties. All your rice...

FIRST SECRETARY. We will hear no more of this treachery. Death to the Dragon!

PENG. No!

GENERAL. Death to the Dragon!

CITIZENS. Death to the Dragon!

(The CITIZENS crowd around the DRAGON, at first cautiously, then, as the DRAGON meekly sinks to his knees in fear, they boldly close in to seize him. The DRAGON crawls out between their legs and leads them in a chase around and about the stage. THEY finally catch him and hold him firmly.)

FIRST SECRETARY. Tie the Dragon to the post until we decide to get rid of him.

(EVERYONE drags the hapless DRAGON to the post. PENG tries to prevent them, but is dragged away, protesting. In a moment the DRAGON is securely tied.)

EMPRESS. The Dragon must die, and also the spy and the traitor.

PENG. Wait! The First Secretary has frightened you with tales of the Dreadful Dragon. But I have found out...

FIRST SECRETARY. This beast and the stranger are working together. They wish to destroy us and take over the Kingdom.

PENG. No! The General and the First Secretary have stolen your rice. They intend to sell it to make themselves rich.

FIRST SECRETARY. How dare you accuse the Royal First Secretary of such a thing! I shall have your head cut off.

GENERAL. *(To the audience.)* I am the Royal General of the Entire Army. Would I do such a thing? *(He may ad lib if the audience responds.)*

FIRST SECRETARY. The stranger lies! Seize him. *(The CITIZENS hold PENG firmly.)*

PENG. I speak the truth. Search the chambers of the First

Secretary. You will find your rice.

FIRST SECRETARY. Would you take the word of a vagabond against that of your own First Secretary?

GENERAL. The stranger knows nothing of our ways.

SOLDIER. Peng speaks the truth, Your Majesties. That is why I let them go.

PENG. We saw them returning from the fields with great baskets of rice.

SOLDIER. They were talking of selling the rice at the market.

GENERAL. The stranger lies. And my army has turned traitor.

PENG. (*To the First Secretary.*) If I do not speak the truth, you cannot object to having your chambers searched.

FIRST SECRETARY. Of course I have no objection. But -- I -- There is no reason, Your Majesty -- there is nothing there -- just a few --

EMPRESS. My Royal First Secretary speaks the truth. Everyone knows that. Herald! Take a citizen and go to the palace. Summon the Royal Executioner.

CITIZENS. Royal Executioner?

EMPRESS. Royal Executioner!

EMPEROR. My dear, isn't that a bit...? (*But SHE silences him with a clap of her hands, followed by a stroke of the GONG. The HERALD selects a CITIZEN and they exit.*)

EMPRESS. When they return, we shall have your heads. It will be a lesson for spies and traitors.

GENERAL. (*Bows to the Empress.*) The Empress is wise. This Dragon is a dangerous beast and must be destroyed.

PENG. But why do you believe the Dragon is dangerous?

EMPRESS. Of course he is dangerous. He will eat all of our good citizens if we do not protect ourselves.

GENERAL. That is what Dragons do.

EMPRESS. Everyone knows that!

EMPEROR. My pet, do you really think...?

EMPRESS. Please do not interfere.

EMPEROR. But it doesn't seem fair.

EMPRESS. I have given the order. The Dragon must die. And spies and traitors as well.

EMPEROR. I don't want them to die.

EMPRESS. I have given the order.

EMPEROR. Well, change the order.

EMPRESS. My mind is made up.

EMPEROR. So is mine.

EMPRESS. But I am the Empress.

EMPEROR. (*Struggles with himself for a moment, then speaks loudly and decisively.*) Well, I am the Emperor. And I say no! (*EVERYONE gasps in amazement, never having heard the Emperor speak so.*)

PENG. (*Suddenly pulls free.*) Wait! I know of a land -- a land where -- when people cannot agree -- they take a VOTE.

EMPRESS. (*With obvious distaste.*) A vote? What manner of a thing is that?

PENG. Why, all those who favor something say "aye," and all those against, say "no." The will of the greatest number wins.

EMPRESS. But when the Empress decides all things, it is so much simpler.

PENG. But when the people decide, it is so much fairer.

EMPEROR. Excellent idea, my Love. We must take a vote at once.

CITIZENS. Yes, yes, a vote. Take a vote.

EMPRESS. (*Reluctantly, she gives in.*) Oh, very well.

(SHE strides around to the CITIZENS as she speaks, cowering them with her glances. The CHILD slowly approaches the DRAGON. HE looks at the Child. Timidly, the CHILD reaches out a hand to pet the DRAGON. HE responds by rubbing against the CHILD. Suddenly, the CHILD's MOTHER sees her so near the DRAGON, gasps in horror, and pulls her away.)

All those in favor of saving our Kingdom from this dreadful, destructive, dangerous Dragon signify by saying "aye."

(Of course, everyone says "aye," the GENERAL and The FIRST SECRETARY voting loudly and repeatedly.)

EMPRESS. There! It's settled.

PENG. Wait. *(Indicates the audience.)* These are the children who walked with me to the edge of the Great Purple Forest when everyone else was afraid. Should they not be allowed to vote?

EMPEROR. Of course. Let the children vote.

FIRST SECRETARY. *(Thinking fast.)* Er -- ah -- children cannot vote.

EMPRESS. Of course. Children cannot vote.

(The CITIZENS huddle to discuss whether children can vote. The EMPRESS claps her hands, silencing the discussion. LAO steps forward.)

LAO. We have decided the children may vote. *(The CITIZENS cheer.)*

PENG. *(Appeals to the audience.)* Children! Please help

us. You have seen the Dragon. You have danced with the Dragon. Now you must save the Dragon. So please, all those who don't want to hurt the Dragon -- who want to save the Dragon -- please -- stand up -- stand up -- and after I count to three -- everybody say NOOOO. As loud as you can. No. Are you ready?

(HE motions the audience to stand. The SOLDIER and CITIZENS help, urging the children to stand up and say "No." The GENERAL and The FIRST SECRETARY motion wickedly to the audience to remain seated.)

All together, now, loud as you can, ONE -- TWO, -- THREE, -- NO!

(The force of the "No" blows everyone over. The EMPRESS falls into the arms of the EMPEROR. The GENERAL falls against the SOLDIER. The CITIZENS fall in various strange positions.)

EMPRESS. *(After everyone recovers.)* I believe -- it was -- it was -- a tie. And in cases of a tie the Empress casts the deciding vote.

CITIZENS. *(Reacting angrily, as it was obviously not a tie.)* A tie! It was not a tie!

EMPRESS. *(Seeing the angry looks.)* Well, perhaps the Dragon had -- just a FEW more votes.

EMPEROR. Release the Dragon!

(The bonds are loosened. There is a shout of joy. The HERALD and the CITIZEN return, carrying the two baskets of rice. Everyone is amazed.)

EMPRESS. What's this?

HERALD. On our way to the palace, we looked into the First Secretary's chamber. And we found these.

CITIZENS. (*Reacting with amazement and anger.*) It is our rice! Peng spoke the truth!

EMPRESS. (*Slowly realizes her terrible mistake.*) I trusted this woman. And she has betrayed my trust. (*To The First Secretary.*) You are no longer my Royal First Secretary.) (*The HERALD confirms this by striking the GONG. The EMPRESS removes the medallion from the FIRST SECRETARY and hangs it on PENG.*) I charge you, as my new Royal First Secretary, to use your office wisely.

PENG. Too great an honor for a stranger, Your Majesty.

EMPRESS. You have shown yourself worthy.

EMPEROR. (*Turns to the General.*) And I see it is time to appoint a new General.

(*Once more the GONG. The EMPEROR removes the GENERAL's sword and hat and with much ceremony, presents them to the SOLDIER. The EMPRESS starts to sit on the upper throne as usual, but the EMPEROR motions her to the lower and takes his place on the upper throne. SHE sits on the lower throne.*)

General! Have that man report!

NEW GENERAL. (*Formerly the SOLDIER.*) Yes, Your Majesty — er, Majesties. Harumph! (*To the SOLDIER, formerly the GENERAL.*) Er, ah — attention! (*The SOLDIER, already at attention, gives a shake and resumes the same position.*) Yes, ah — report!

SOLDIER. (*With great importance.*) Sir, I have nothing to report!

GENERAL. Any sign of the -- ah -- enemy?

SOLDIER. (*HE looks about the stage carefully, finally looking directly at the Dragon.*) No, Sir!

GENERAL. Excellent. Now, Your Majesty, what shall we do about the Dragon?

CITIZENS. Yes, what will we do about the Dragon?

EMPEROR. I know. It was the children who saved the Dragon. And the children who love the Dragon. And he certainly loves the children. So I shall appoint the Dragon -- The Emperor's Royal -- PLAYMATE OF THE CHILDREN!

(*A great cheer goes up. The DRAGON does a little dance for joy, then goes to PENG.*)

PENG. Take good care of the children, my friend.

ALL. (*Singing.*)
AND NOW WE'VE SAVED OUR DRAGON,
JUST SEE HIS TAIL A-WAGGIN'.

(*Obligingly, the DRAGON shakes his rear end, and his tail wags.*)

EMPRESS. (*Interrupting the song.*) My dear Citizens, as your Empress, I have labored tirelessly to save the life of this dear, sweet, little --

ALL.
AND NOW WE'VE SAVED OUR DRAGON,
JUST SEE HIS TAIL A-WAGGIN'.

(*Again the DRAGON obliges.*)

PENG. As your Royal First Secretary, my every thought

has been for justice. I am pleased to inform you that our
beloved Dragon --
    ALL.
AND NOW WE'VE SAVED OUR DRAGON,
JUST SEE HIS TAIL A-WAGGIN'.

    *(The DRAGON gives a sigh of weariness, but wags his
    tail once more.)*

    GENERAL. As General of your entire army --
    SOLDIER. And as your entire army --
    ALL.
AND NOW WE'VE SAVED OUR DRAGON,
JUST SEE HIS TAIL A-WAGGIN'.

    (The DRAGON makes a gesture as if to say "forget it!")

HE'LL BE OUR FRIEND, SO THIS IS THE END

    (THEY pick up the DRAGON for the final line.)

OF OUR TALE ABOUT THE DRAGON!
HE'LL BE OUR FRIEND, SO THIS IS THE END,
OF OUR TALE ABOUT THE DRAGON!

    *(THEY put the DRAGON down. HE dances up the
    aisle and into the lobby to give the children a good-bye
    hug as THEY leave the theatre.)*

* * *

ABOUT PARTICIPATION PLAYS

Charlotte Chorpenning has observed that no child's body was made to sit still long enough to watch a play. She always wrote into her plays a series of "anti-fidget" devices -- chase scenes, fights, large movements from one end of the stage to the other. These caused the children to jump up and down with excitement or to follow the action by moving their bodies in response to the actor's movement.

She wrote her plays for five year-olds and older. When a play is presented with children as young as three or four in the audience, the problem is compounded. One solution is to give the young ones an opportunity to get out of their seats and DO something. After this exercise they can relax and lose themselves again in the play.

But there is another reason for audience participation. A child's natural play consists mainly of *play acting*, of pretending, of doing what actors do. In the theatre they are suddenly asked to sit passively and watch someone else play-act. For a three year-old, this is a major transition. But by placing the audience in the cast, by asking them to join in the play-acting, we form a bridge between childlike play and mature theatre attendance.

In a participation play, actors learn to PLAY with their audiences, to accept them as part of the story, to improvise dialogue and action, whenever necessary, in response to the children's spontaneous reactions. In short, the "fourth wall" of the set is no longer a proscenium arch, but the back wall of the auditorium.

Names and Places

Although strict authenticity is not imperative in children's fantasy plays, the use of a dragon frequently suggests China. I have therefore used Chinese names. The Citizens have not been given strongly delineated characters, as I wanted the effect of an anthill, with everyone seemingly dashing helter-skelter without organization or plan.

I did find, however, that telling the actors the meanings of their names helped them develop some feeling of character.

Chan: To Give Birth to.
Sheng: Angry.
Tsung: Clever.

Lao: Ancient.
Hai: Fearful.
Peng: Friend.

Properties List

Two thrones
Banner or Sign on a post
Three Swords
Medallion on a chain
Chinese gong
Scroll
Trees on stands
Two large baskets filled with rice on the ends of a pole
[Styrofoam packing can be used for rice.]
Length of rope.

About the Playwright

Burt Liebert earned a Master of Fine Arts in Theatre from Chicago Art Institute. At Goodman Theatre, Chicago, he worked for three years in the children's theatre company of Charlotte Chorpenning. He then became director of Southwest Players, and adult community theatre specializing in plays for children. He was a teacher of high school drama for twelve years and a lecturer at the University of California for sixteen years. He is now devoting himself to writing plays for young audiences.

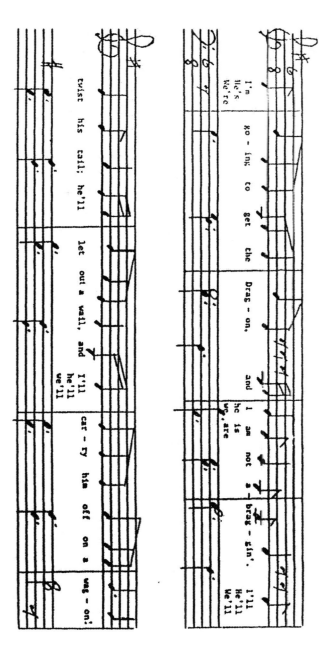

GOING TO GET THE DRAGON

I'm go - ing to get the Drag - on, and I am not a - brag - gin'.
He's
We're

twist his tail; he'll let out a wall, and I'll car - ry him off on a wag - on!
he'll
we'll

And now we've saved our Dragon,
Just see his tail a-waggin'.
He'll be our friend, so this is the end
Of our tale about the Dragon!

POOR ME

Poor me! Poor me! O - h see my mis - er - y; To
I see, th - is is the end of me! To
Poor me! Poor me! O - h see my mis - er - y; To

face that beast would take at least a hun - dred in - fan - try;
face that beast would take at least a thou - sand cav - al - ry;
face that beast would take at least some huge ar - til - ler - y;

OTHER TITLES AVAILABLE FROM BAKER'S PLAYS

OLIVER TWIST

Brian Way

18m, 3f, or as low as 5m or 3f with doubling

A straightforward version of Dickens' classic, set in 19th Century London, in which young Oliver runs away from an orphanage and is taken by the Artful Dodger to Fagin's den, where he joins in a series of adventures with Fagin's street gang until he is befriended by Mr. Brownlow. An honest, loving and exciting adaptation. For all ages.

OTHER TITLES AVAILABLE FROM BAKER'S PLAYS

ALICE IN AMERICA-LAND
or *Through the Picture Tube and What Alice Found There*

Dennis Snee

Comedy Fantasy / Flexible / Open Stage with Backdrops

In this fresh and lively update of Lewis Carroll's classic, Alice takes a journey through the picture tube of her family's television, and meets a mad collection of characters — with a certain difference! A White Rabbit — who lives in fear of someone's dropping "the big one." A Mock Turtle — who's a champion of consumer rights. A Dodo who's a guitarist, a Dormouse seeking political office and an Eagle who lives in the past. The Duke and Duchess have switched life roles — she's a "working duchess" while he's a "house duke." Alice herself becomes the unwitting subject for a showbiz roast with two aging, bitter comedians — the Mad Hatter and the March Hare. Through it all, Alice just wants to return home to her beloved cat. Just when it seems as though this mad world of America-land will drive her as mad as the inhabitants, she awakens, safe at home, her cat in her lap. A fanciful, biting, always funny tale of a contemporary Alice that will delight all audiences.